The Anatomy of a Heartbreak

A COLLECTION OF POEMS

NANCY SAGE

Dedicated to:

My "a lot, a lot."

How strange it is,

    To oscillate between

Anger & Depression;

    Hope & Belonging.

Contents
The Anatomy of a Heartbreak

Foreword

To have heartbreak is to be human. No one person will experience it in quite the same way. I think it is most useful to consider heartbreak through the stages of grief; but everyone's grief is different. Not everyone will experience every stage, some stages are shorter than others. One almost always goes into and out of the stages fluidly as opposed to chronologically.

The following collection of poems are organized by grief stage, though I did not experience the grief from my own heartbreak in such a structured way. As a reader, I encourage you to open to a section that speaks to you instead of reading cover to cover.

Some sections are longer than others. Indeed, some sections barely exist at all for I experienced little of these stages. But I hope this is comforting—to know that there is no "right way" to experience grief when your heart is breaking. You just have to sit in it. But you will get through it.

-N.S.

Shock & Denial

If we can deny that something is happening, we don't have to sit in the hurt. We can avoid the pain and the shame that comes from the decision.

Yet our mind is smarter than this. We cannot stay in denial for long. If we do, we risk living in two separate realities—in our mind and in our physical space. The soul suffers when living in this in between.

So, deny it for as long as you need, but remember that true healing will start when you accept your reality and sit in the hurt.

Love me—I plead.

But love refuses to negotiate with me.

Confusion compounds me.

Two feelings.

Two choices.

Two desires.

Two questions.

Yet when duality and contradiction are present in one—

Rationality and intelligence give way to raw emotion.

We are at War.

A war of words,

to win the mind.

Truth wallows.

Lies cackle.

We must win to survive.

But how can we survive with all the lies?

What a funny thing it is—reason versus yearning.

For I know that which would be good for me,

And yet,

This is the one I least desire.

Sometimes I wish I could escape inside my mind.

Go frolic in my fantasies,

relive my memories.

and dive into my imaginations.

The world is nicer there.

There is laughter and love and joy,

in ways never possible here.

But maybe purity and rawness of pain and hurt and fear

is what makes the honey of the mind taste so delicious.

For without spice and bitterness,

the sweetness of honey would be unknown.

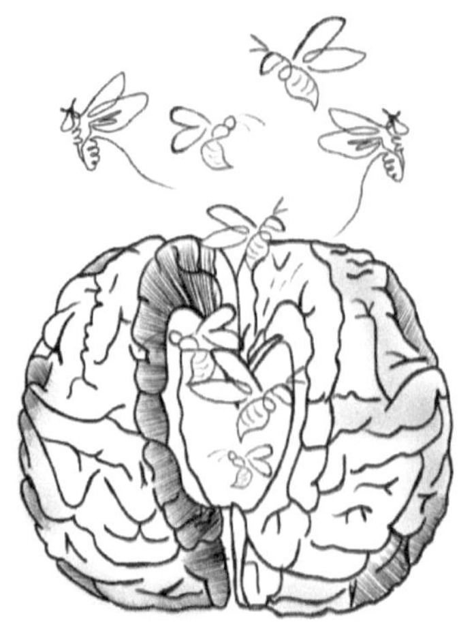

At some point, heartbreak will hit you. Whether you believe it is the right decision or not, whether you made the move or received it, whether you have all the best distractions and support or none; heartbreak and raw pain will hit you like a freight train and force you to stop everything. It will make you sit in the emotion. You will be forced to wallow.

This is one of the hardest stages to get through. All hope seems lost. The apathy for life is palpable and fierce. But sit in it. Feel it. Experience it. You must, in order to move on.

Love is a fickle thing.

You let it in, and if you are lucky,

it fades like the seeds of an aged dandelion.

But alas, more oft than not,

it rots from the stem.

Death and disease follow.

Love, you fickle thing,

Be gone and don't come back.

There is a grey storm brewing in my body.

I feel it everywhere within me.

It never goes away,

But never erupts either.

It just brews, forever enveloping

my body in darkness.

The loss of possibility is the worst grief of all,

Because hope idealizes reality.

My body yearns for what my mind knows it needs not

I long for the day when my mind is stronger than my body,

for when the body wins the match,

the mind suffers the most with bruises and blows.

He doesn't want me anymore.

Empty.

He doesn't love me anymore.

Worthless.

He doesn't care about me anymore.

Disaster.

Grief shows up at my doorstep.

I let her in, even though I knew what she could bring.

We sat and chatted like old friends,

but I could feel her pull.

She wanted to stay.

I, stoic, showed her to the door.

She left devastated. I? numb.

And now here I am. In my house,

that no longer feels like home.

Muting my feelings, so Grief doesn't show up again.

But I know eventually, she will ring the doorbell

and I'll have to answer it.

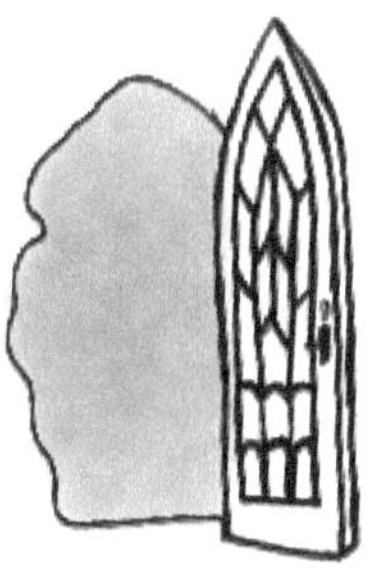

I think miscommunication is the root of all man's evil.

Ignorance wears a wedding gown.

Flittering down the aisle with ballet slippers

to not break the egg shells.

A veil drawn to keep out the truth.

So happy—is she—

unaware and feeling free.

And the guests smile on

taking photo after photo,

capturing this moment that is but a fleeting dream.

The photos I place in my box jump to life;

Showing a snapshot of glorious days,

of have beens and yesteryears;

Of a time when there was such hope for a joyous future,

But alas, a photo knows only the outward appearance,

it sees not the inner turmoil

of the soul screaming.

There is an empty void ripping me apart from the inside.

My heart goes first,

Followed by my chest,

Then my stomach—

All falling into this black hole.

Until I feel as though there is nothing left.

I've been crying so much,

I could supply a thousand droughts.

My heart, my soul, is dark

like the night sky.

Void and empty of anything.

The darkness suffocates me;

Blackness is all around.

Time will pass.

The moon will come back.

Light will fill the dark.

Patience.

It will brighten the night yet again.

I have one night stands with self-loathing,

over and over again.

When I'm sad and alone, I call her here,

to join me in bed.

My body feels raped by her,

when the night is through.

In the moment, there is pleasure in the pain.

So I'll invite her back again,

Unwelcomed.

Living together rips me apart from the inside.

He looks at me with a mixture of

love, contempt, desire, and disgust.

How should we act?

What should we say?

How can you face the man you fell out of love with

Every single day?

Sin. Forgive. Rinse. Repeat.

Sin. Rinse. Forgive. Repeat.

Rinse. Sin. Repeat. Forgive.

Sin. Rinse. Repeat.

No longer forgive.

I pack the boxes from a past life,

reliving every memory as I place items delicately

one on top of the other;

I'm transported to the hot summer day

holding your hand as my present self grasps the fabric of
the dress I wore;

I jump into the picture of I on your back, head thrown
back

Laughing

As my present self grips the photo;

I fold your sweaters, smelling for any small trace of you
left,

my present self wishing to be with you once more,

But alas,

there was joy in the memories

but pain in the present, and my present self knows

I can never go back.

We fought long and hard;

always putting in a valiant effort.

The Great War was ours to win.

But you lost your will to fight,

and soon I did too,

and what was once our Great War to win

became a Great War to fight.

Me against You.

And now it's over,

and no one has won, have they?

We both lost the War;

And are lost without it.

It's a common trope:

Strangers, Friends, Lovers, Strangers again.

But makes one wonder,

If you can so easily go back to strangers,

what does that say about the love to begin with?

I watched as you chose someone else to do life with
you.

I cried myself to sleep thinking how your chest

would be a pillow for someone else.

I saw someone invade and replace me in your life,

and the internal turmoil I felt,

was nothing short of war;

For I knew we should not be together,

And yet,

My body yearned for you so much more than before.

Heartbreak fuels idiocy.

We are martyrs.

One after the other.

Taking blame on the shoulders,

believing self destruction is the only way.

So we lie in wake.

And then do it all again;

Martyrdom comes at a cost,

when is it too much for you?

You are always better for the next one,

Aren't you?

The pain is strong when I see you being the

man I wanted,

for Her.

But if I wasn't worth it then,

why should I believe that I would be worth it to you
now?

How strange it is,

that when one offers solutions,

we feel even more alone.

Pain and turmoil flow like a river through my body.

Splashing over rocks of insecurity

that held the bed for so long.

Waterflowing down years of trauma and memories.

Twisting and turning around doubt and fear.

Emptying into a sea of nothingness.

If all rivers connect to this

vastless body,

why flow at all?

The worst part about leaving your love,

is no longer having someone with whom

to share your life's revelations.

I, like a little girl, desire security, safety, and protection.

I need these things, I say.

How do you know you need them,

if you have never experienced them before? You ask.

Wallowing in the pain

empties the soul.

It's contagiously addicting,

yet has limited benefit

beyond the first

drunken remorse.

It fills one with pity

and shame takes over quickly.

So think hard if you want to let wallowing in

once more.

My pain for the loss of you is visceral.

The loss of what our life could have been.

The loss of an idolized future.

It's so strong, this pain,

I began to forget how you made me feel,

and why I left in the first place.

But if I go back, it will be a jarring reality,

Won't it?

For ideals are for those that live in the clouds,

and I'm ready to live with my feet on the ground

for the first time in my life.

The body hates the in-between;

It desires a resolve;

Yet to sit in the in-between is when the soul starts to speak

with great fervor.

So be still, and be patient,

and listen for the voice;

Your soul will be screaming soon enough.

I want to take refuge in the water,

have it swallow me whole,

baptize me new,

cleanse me of these toxic thoughts,

to be made pure again,

and look at the world as does a babe—

with curiosity and wonder and hope.

The worst pain is that in which you know it's for the best,

Yet it destroys you on the inside.

No amount of rationalizing can take the heart break away.

Try not, my love, for you will only hurt yourself in attempting.

No, tis better to feel the worst pain of your life,

For pain builds strength

and strength builds resilience

and resilience builds confidence.

Stay the course.

Stay the course.

Pain can give way to anger. Anger for decisions made, anger for a lost future, anger for lies.

Although grief is not chronological, I believe when you finally get angry, it is a good sign that you are on the precipice of a new beginning.

Thank you for reminding me who you are,

I had forgotten yet again,

and almost let you step over my boundaries,

just like before.

But I saw you for who you are,

and I finally felt anger—

an anger I can turn into action.

So watch out,

because I am done being taken advantage of by you.

Running, fast, far, anywhere.

Take me away.

I can't stay here;

Stuck, stagnant, spiraling head first into the same
mistakes.

I run.

Running far, anywhere.

Just take me from this place.

I need to leave.

Self destructive, idiotic, diving into the deep end of
regret.

I run.

Running anywhere.

Let me go.

I have to escape.

Trapped, hopeless, stepping further

into the land of dejection.

I run.

Running,

From what I've become.

Me and second chances go way back;

Like a puppy whining at the door,

I let him in, time and time again.

He promised I would never see him after the time
before.

Yet he keeps showing up.

And I keep welcoming him.

"Hello, second chance, nice to meet you."

When will I realize He at my door is not second chance
any longer?

For I've met second, third, fourth, fifth...

chance before.

And he will keep walking through my door.

Betrayal wears a sports coat.

It speaks the words you are desperate to hear—

But lo! You know its motives are never quite clear.

It whispers promises that hug your anxiety;

And yet, what a relief when it no longer comes back.

You never showed me what love looked like.

How was I to know?

That love shouldn't be hard;

That love cannot be obtained with a checklist,

That love does not always make sense.

Maybe if you had taught me,

I wouldn't have gotten so hurt.

A fire was raging inside of me.

I finally let it out,

And now

I feel as though I am combusting.

But it worries me not.

For I believe when the flames die out,

I will still be standing.

There may be burns, and cuts, and bruises.

But I survived *that*.

And no one can take such a power away.

You're welcome—future lover of his.

He put me through so much pain,

So he knows better for you.

I told him what hurt,

So he can change before you.

We created shared trauma,

So he won't do so with you.

You're welcome—future lover of his—

For turning him into the man of my dreams,

Just in time for you.

Anger and grief are in a tug of war

I, the referee, watch with baited breath.

Anger pulls hard, shouting "Why, why why?!"

Grief tugs back croaking, "oh why, why, why?"

The deadlock remains.

The flag won't budge.

Both anger and grief are equal in strength.

Who holds the power? Who will win?

I blow the whistle.

"Times up," I cry.

"Why, Why, Why;"

"Oh why, why, why?"

I look them over one last time.

"Because I'm done with this game and must get on."

Bang. Bang.

The knock on the door from the girl you once knew.

Bang. Bang.

Convincing yourself no one will know but you.

Bang. Bang.

Your heart thumps in your chest.

Bang. Bang.

Pulsing blood into all of your extremities.

Bang. Bang.

You respond when your friends ask how your night went.

Bang. Bang.

Laughing at your egotistical success.

Bang. Bang.

Your bullet of betrayal shot me through the heart.

Bang. Bang.

Shattering my perception of reality.

Bang. Bang.

Your fist through the wall as you realize what you've done.

Bang. Bang.

Claiming it's a mistake that'll never happen again.

Bang. Bang.

The gavel sounds at the court finalizing our divorce.

Bang. Bang.

Freeing myself of your childish games forever more.

Bang. Bang.

My heels as I loudly walk away turning my back on you.

Bang. Bang.

I refuse to let you have the last word.

There comes a point when you feel ready to move on. You realize you can make it. You may even start down this path. But inevitably, something happens that scares you. You get hurt and battered for starting down this new path, so you doubt your ability.

You want to go back to predictability. For even if it was not good in the moment, you knew what to expect. Predictability is safe, and we like safety in our lives. So you start believing your past life wasn't so bad, that the safety of predictability is worth any pain and suffering.

But just remember—this feeling is exactly where you are supposed to be. If you start to get uncomfortable, it means you are moving out of your comfort zone into where real growth can start. Don't go back. Forge ahead.

Regret raps on my door, in the freezing of the night.

I let him in and serve him tea.

We sit across from one another,

silence weighing heavy over us.

The steam from the mugs warms the cold distance

I feel between him and I.

He brings a blanket over, and drapes it over my
shoulder.

I place my hand in his as he leads me into the bedroom.

I cuddle with regret for I hope it will bring me warmth.

But regret stays cold,

And the closer I snuggle into him,

the more my body loses heat.

For regret just takes,

And if I'm not careful,

Regret will take all of me.

Hidden secrets,

Dark lies,

Sneaky rendezvous,

The thrill, the danger, the desire.

Intoxicating.

It's a drug, an addiction, a crime.

But eventually, the bond will snap.

For two negatives will always push apart.

When the world sleeps, I stir.

Haunted by torments of yet to comes.

The soul yearns for an answer;

But the heart and mind remain in fierce battle.

I must release my fear,

Then I too can slumber under the stars.

Life is a series of decisions.

Our minds think hard and say yes or no.

And each decision has consequences.

But if we let our decisions be dictated by trauma,

are we ever really in control?

Feelings betray my mind.

I long for you, for us,

Even when I know it to not be best.

My body became so used to tucking itself into yours,

It yearns to be snapped back together again.

But I will sit in the pain,

And let my mind win,

Even though everything inside me

Feels like it is being ripped from within.

For short term pleasure

will lead to long term disappointment.

I almost went back to him,

That man that made love hard.

I could have difficult love forever,

Every day.

But I'll wait an eternity for a love that feels easy.

At some point, you will start to test what a new life could look like. Perhaps you begin dating and see what a loving relationship could feel like.

You test yourself by being with other people—can you do it? Can they do it? It is necessary for healing. But while this stage may seem fun at first, there will be pain in it too.

For you can't start a new love journey until you have finally accepted what happened with your last.

Enjoy the steps, but tread carefully. Soon one "he" will turn into many and you may be left more heartbroken than before.

Desire—

He's come for me.

He teases my temptations.

He heats my soul.

Desire—

He's extended his hand to me.

I pass over my self control.

I surrender my breath.

Desire—

He's taken me.

You live your life,

So used to seeing Red,

Red faces burning with anger,

Red blood coursing through you from a fight,

Red flags warning you to reconsider;

That to not see Red

starts to feel dangerous.

I crave chaos.

The unexpected, the drama, the rush of adrenaline.

It fills me with fire.

But the chaos comes at a cost.

And soon I'll be too weak to pay.

There are times I flirt with bad ideas,

I grind on the same mistakes,

I make out with the patterns,

And I let the red flags hump me in bed.

I know this, yet I still flirt and dance and cuddle.

And once I finally let go, I know I will be met with

Kind words

And slow dances

Soft kisses

And warm cuddles.

But until then,

I live and love in the chaos I've created.

I asked distraction to take me out,

for a night on the town.

We danced and laughed hour after hour.

I forgot my pain as Distraction spun me

around the dance floor.

The night ended and Distraction walked me to my door;

As I closed it behind me,

I wondered why I felt worse than before.

There is safety in predictability,

To knowing how every action will be received.

Because I knew you inside out.

I read your book front to back,

Can recite the memorized lines.

Yet you never wanted to read mine.

So I've given my book over to a new lover, and he the same to me.

And while there are times I turn the page

And am met with surprise,

At least he is reading alongside of me.

You are the reader of my book.

Take pride, because I don't give it away often.

The beginning is shit—be forewarned.

The middle is powerful, full of surprises.

Yet I'm stuck finishing the book.

I keep turning back, copying and pasting old pages.

Will you help me with the ending?

I forgot what joy felt like,

And I found it sitting among the wild flowers.

A butterfly flew by and showed me the way.

To a world I was living in, but not fully seeing.

For when you open your heart to nature's beauty,

It will find you where you least expect it.

And take you to a majestic place.

Full of wonder and happiness.

You need only follow the butterfly.

We are two leaves blowing in the breeze.

Letting the wind take us this way and that.

I'm not sure where I will land, nor do you.

But I'm enjoying being in this jet stream,

Together, for now.

And if the wind makes us cross paths again,

I'll enjoy that moment too,

And I'll know that our floating together

was not happenstance,

rather it is nature telling us there is

something special here.

But for now,

let us just float side by side

until our winds take us separate ways.

My soul met yours on a late summer night.

When the trees were still and the world was asleep.

They danced together under the moonlit sky;

Becoming one in little time.

Yet the world is a cruel and dark place

when the sun rises over the horizon.

For our souls must part ways as daybreak gives way;

Not out of want, but of need.

My soul, though, is not inquieted.

For our night-time rendezvous nourishes my famishment

Until our next encounter in the night.

Our companionship is a siren song,

Pulling us in, intoxicating us.

Intense and overwhelming,

Passionate, pure, and raw.

It drowns out everything else,

And makes us want more.

"Come deeper in," it calls.

If we aren't careful, it will suck us in,

Stupefying us with a connection

So strong, so understood,

it could have only come from the gods.

But leaving a shipwreck in its wake.

We met as fireflies in the morning—

Unsure and skeptical to show each other our light—

Afraid of what would happen

if we tried to illuminate the daytime.

For we had been trapped before,

when we shone our light to others.

But we were released from captivity—

Of the mind and body—

Free to fly once more.

And there we met.

We flew side by side

Caught in one another's wind streams,

Happy for companionship.

And as dusk was beginning, you flickered,

And I back;

Trusting that the light would be safe this time.

Yours with me, and mine with you.

And how lucky it was, to trust, to shine,

For now we are dancing in the night,

Shining brighter than before,

All because of a flicker.

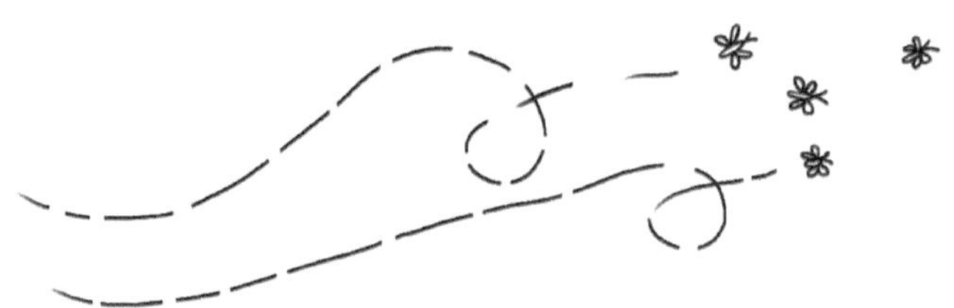

I'm sorry for making the same mistakes over and over

These actions have been reinforced

after years of abuse.

I seek to win your love with actions.

Yet, the most loving thing may be to do nothing at all.

Shame and I go a long way back.

She whispers delicacies in my ear,

making me think she knows exactly what I

Want, Need, Desire.

She'll set me up on blind dates,

watching with delight as I take the bait.

For what she offers feels to me

so deserving.

To be a seashell,

Tossed around by a great force;

Discarded after no longer being wanted;

Crushed under the weight of others around you.

But then picked up as a treasure to someone new.

Lo! To be a seashell

Is to be but a human.

Validation is my captor.

Handcuffing me to past trauma.

I know I shouldn't like it,

But the Stockholm syndrome is strong,

And I enjoy my captor.

He makes me feel seen and important.

But my captor is not safe;

For validation will always desire me to stay a prisoner.

And it's finally time for me to start craving freedom.

I wonder if unrequited love is better than forbidden love.

At least in one, you slowly lose hope.

Have you ever tried holding sand in your hand? He asked

The harder you squeeze, the more gets released.

I'm your sand, he continued.

Trust that I won't leave,

If you hold onto me gently.

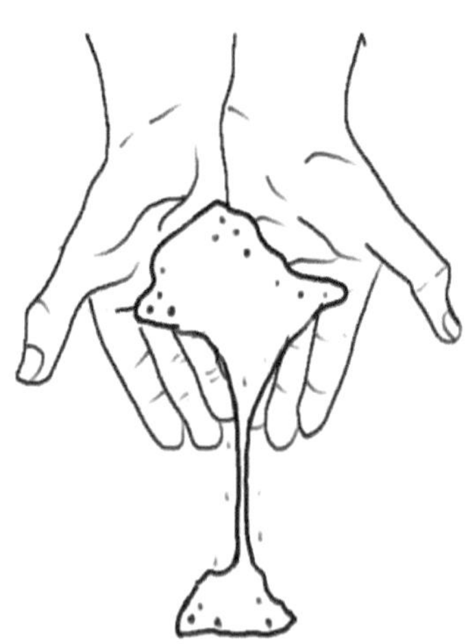

Heartache and Heartbreak meet

Butterflies and Warmth rising.

Empty and Numb open the door to

Joy and Laughter.

Hope follows in the shadows of Grief.

A paradox of emotions is to

Be Human.

When I see the moon,

I think of you.

Worlds apart,

We connect at night.

Two souls touching,

With stars as our witness.

We need not speak,

For I know what you see, and you I.

And knowing that you think of me too,

When you see the moon,

Will get me through.

I cried leaving you.

You thought I was sad to be out of your presence;

Not knowing when I would see you again;

But in fact,

I was sobbing

Because I had never felt so loved before,

And the thought of willingly leaving such a gift,

Was blasphemy to my heart.

My body yearns for you

when you are not here.

A tingling of my soul,

being separated from her other half.

And when you are near,

my body knows.

I go weak in the knees

and wet between the thighs,

For when we two collide,

our worlds will once again be made whole.

Seduction is addicting, isn't it?

The dopamine hits. 1. 2. 3.

It tickles your thrill.

Yet you always feel worse after, don't you?

For you didn't have enough strength to resist.

And you know this,

Every time you decide to try again.

Yet it calls you back.

And you listen.

Why?

Because you aren't yet strong enough

To know that you are better than that.

And you deserve more

Than addiction has to offer.

I see him from a distance.

Something turns in my stomach.

That look, that glance.

I know it well.

A chance encounter, and I'll never be the same.

Obsession.

I long for him and all he has.

That kiss, that touch, I dream of it often.

An explosion of passion, and I'll never be the same.

Desire.

I feel like he can mend my broken child within.

That reassurance, that love I've wanted all my life.

It's so much so fast, so we will never be the same.

Acceptance.

I must love myself first for my child to be healed.

That self love, that care, and I'll never be the same.

And therefore, neither will we.

No, we will be better.

The difference between my past and him.

He reassures even when speaking harsh truths.

My past spoke harsh truths to hurt.

He worships my body,

My past used my body.

He believes I deserve to be loved,

My past believed I must earn love.

He feels safe,

My past feels dangerous, now.

Temptation sneaks up on you,

Whispering delicacies in your ear;

Feathering fingertips across the back of your neck,

Inviting you to follow her for more.

Resist her if you can,

But she knows all your deepest secrets

and what you need;

So will you let her tempt you?

There's only one way to find out.

Give in to her danger,

if you are brave enough,

and have your soul rocked from within.

But beware,

For Temptation comes from the darkness,

fueled by one's inner demons and desires.

I crawl back into old mistakes,

Bad habits, and forgone paths travelled before,

Expecting a different result,

For they are disguised as new fun toys,

Yet they always end the same;

For although each new time is slightly different than the last,

They all share one commonality—

Unavailability—

Allowing me to never question the deep belief within myself—

Unworthy—

For finally choosing to walk a different path,

And accepting more,

Runs counter to years of conditioning, predictability,

Even though this is the very thing keeping the good

Forever out of my grasp.

I walk in a circle.

Finally feeling as though I am making progress,

Only to find I'm back where I started.

A new time around,

But same start and end.

If only I could find a way off.

Double heartbreak is a special thing;

You have one,

So you attempt to mend it by finding a solution,

A quick fix to make you feel whole and worthy inside;

But this inevitably ends in a conflagration

Much earlier, yet like the initial.

And now you are left with a double heart break,

When you should have just managed the first.

I came to you in a time of need;

I pretended I was fine and quickly gave you the key

to all things holy in me;

You tried your best but were set up for an impossible feat,

For I needed to be my own locksmith

before I ever handed over to you my keys.

I used you as a raft,

When I didn't trust myself to swim.

A life jacket would have sufficed,

But it felt good to lay on the deck

And sun bathe my way through life.

But I drowned when a storm blew its way across the
ocean,

And the raft was no more,

And my biggest regret is trying to use the raft

to cross the ocean.

When it would have been better

to enjoy the sun

and gentle rock of the water

on the raft, later on.

My pain over the mistake I made with you

grows more intense by the day.

Time is the enemy of the soul,

and I wish I waited

before inviting you in

to the dungeon masquerading as a cozy bedroom,

that was my heart.

To open your heart to love,

Is to invite uncertainty,

Is to invite possible pain,

Is to invite hurt, loss, and grief.

But to not open your heart to love at all,

Hurts far greater.

Rejection stings like an awful sunburn.

You try to continue going about your life,

But the pain hits you every time you start getting comfortable.

And you can try and soothe the burning sensation,

But this normally only offers temporary relief.

Alas, you must wait.

And eventually the red hot throbbing pain

Will be replaced with more protection for you than before,

A healthy glow, and learned lessons for the future.

How brave you have been in life, to make it here. Take pride in your feat. It wasn't easy. But now, you can feel stronger and more sure of yourself. You can do it—you can do life.

Souls live in the inbetween.

The in between of physical and metaphysical.

The in between of logic and emotion.

And therefore when two souls connect,

You often don't know what hit you.

But I know what it feels like.

It feels safe and authentic.

Vulnerable and trusting.

Like home and heaven all at once.

So I choose to live and walk in my soul,

Even if it makes me different,

For I'd rather live whole than anything else.

Footsteps follow me.

Indentations in the ground,

Showing me where I once walked.

Haunting—they are.

Allowing me to go back and relive any trial once tread.

I've run from them for so long—

Always forward, faster still.

Yet today, I looked behind me.

And they were not there.

Alas, the ocean had swept away all remnants of my once near distant past.

And for once, I finally felt free.

How beautiful it is to have a still mind.

To be struck by a thought, a feeling,

an image so pure, so raw, so intense,

that the mind can do nothing,

but go silent;

so as to not take away from the marvel that is in front of
you.

Don't let go of happiness.

It's becoming all too rare these days.

The road to recovery is long and winding,

Like highway 1.

If you try to forge straight ahead,

You will no doubt lose your traction and slide

into the vast ocean below.

But if you follow the curves

and take your time,

you will eventually make it to your destination.

Do you know each time you left,

You tore a part of me?

Each time you laid with a woman,

A small part of me died?

With every lie,

My identity was slowly chipped away

Until there was barely anything left.

Now I don't know who I am,

But I am ready to find out.

I used to think, if I had all the answers, I wouldn't get hurt.

But in my quest for answers,

I realized,

The greatest beauty comes from not knowing,

and trusting that going into the dark unknown

will bring light and beauty

beyond any answer that could be discovered.

Sitting here, I feel small;

And what a glorious feeling to have.

My existence matters little

In this great big world.

There's beauty in letting go.

In realizing that the planet will continue turning,

The sun will rise and fall again,

The ocean waves will crash into shore tomorrow

as they did today.

My problems are just that—mine.

And it is I who give them power,

For no one else, nothing else,

Will be as affected by them as me.

She looks out the wire bars that contain her,

At a world so full of wonder and possibilities.

Imagining the day when the door is opened,

For she will fly away.

Out in the world, she soars.

Climbing to new heights she never thought possible.

The door has been opened,

She is never going back.

But the world is dark and cruel,

She didn't know how hunted she would be.

The trap was sweetened with honey,

Masquerading the danger.

Trapped now, she wails,

Wallowing in her own misfortune,

Yearning for the old cage once again.

But she remembers flying at night toward the moon,

And she is not the same as before.

For the man in the moon told her she was a Phoenix,

and convinced her that the fire and flames are surmountable.

So she burned,

Trusting the man in the moon,

That she would rise stronger out of the ashes.

I ran toward a goal.

Target, prep, aim.

Success was easy.

Yet not once did I stop and ask,

"Is this the right goal?"

Now I'm running fast from it,

And finding I can no longer compete as I once did,

For while everyone else learned how to

Target, prep, aim better;

I was enjoying a prize I didn't want.

I must move on,

And learn to love myself.

But how can I when I know nothing but you?

I must be content alone,

But how can I when you have always been around?

I must gain self confidence and courage,

But how can I when you kept me in a box?

To get from where I am to where I am going,

I must lose you.

To go from where you are to where you want to be is painful.

Do you love me?

It's a question always on my mind.

How can I make you love me?

I answer with strategies to make it so.

I think love is a game that can be won,

There are winners and losers.

And if I try hard enough, I will always come out on top.

But now I'm losing the game,

And with it, my identity.

And I realize love is not a game,

It just Is.

And there are not winners and losers,

Just people.

And the only way to truly win,

Is to win the game of love with yourself.

So here I go;

Game, set, match.

There are many places we can choose to live:

In the heart, the mind, the body, the soul.

The heart will send you a million directions,

Craving validation and love from anyone who will give it.

The mind will scorn and repel and make you doubt yourself,

It will use logic to run circles around you.

The body will ask you to live in the moment,

But also distract you from the rest of life if you let it.

But the soul is different.

The soul sees people for who they really are,

And extends a hand out in connection.

So I choose to live in the soul.

For although it may feel intense and uncomfortable at first,

I'd much rather see the world for what it truly is

And touch authenticity with vulnerability and acceptance.

Only then can you feel at peace.

You cannot rebuild what was never there to begin with.

Push forward when you don't want to,

Put one foot in front of the other

Even when you feel lost;

Take a deep breath when your body is caving in;

Ball your fists, raise your head, stare with resolve,

For this too shall pass,

And the person on the other side is waiting for you;

One small step is all you need to take.

There lies beauty in the brokenness,

In the pain and the shame.

For when we give in to our shadows,

Our body and soul fuse to ignite.

And though it may be fleeting and

Ephemeral at best,

There is not a beauty so pure as that

With the darkness.

So I will give in, until my last breath.

It's easy to follow a path,

The path that has been laid out for you

By so many before.

To walk along and not question why,

You'll probably be happier for it too.

Yes, much harder is it to step off that path,

To question why and for what and how.

No, it may not be the path to happiness,

But what is promised is even better—

Fulfillment, understanding, and self acceptance.

So step off the path,

And join us in reclaiming your life.

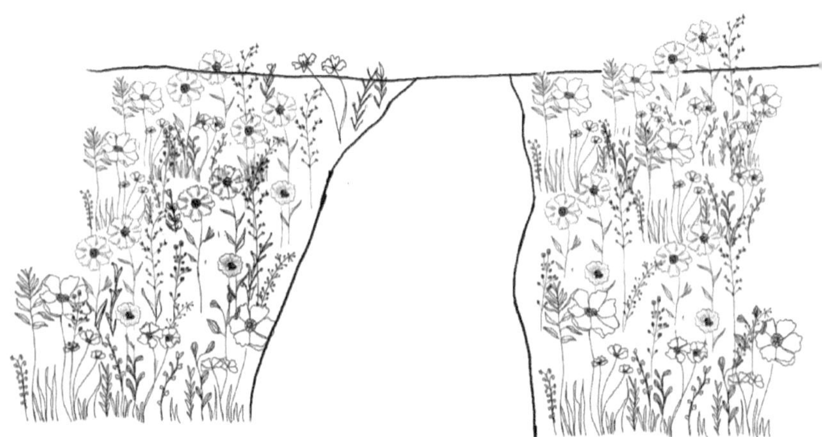

I am filled with the strength of thousands of women

Who have walked before

I stand on their shoulders,

Climbing to these new heights,

Unafraid to say no,

Unafraid to be me.

I've been told I'm too much,

Too intense,

Too emotional,

Too much feeling,

Too much affection,

Too over the top,

Too much attention.

But I finally realized,

I'm not too much;

I was just too much for you.

The end of an era is a happy sad.

And that's okay.

A powerful rebirth consumes my being.

It's been dormant, waiting for this moment.

And now that it is here,

It can't be put back,

Wrapped up, packaged with a bow tie like before—

Always told to stay put and not come out.

No.

Here you are, the powerful fire within me.

And I'll never let you be put away again.

"What is a soul?" I ask.

"Our connection to the universe," he answers.

I hold self discovery's hand,

For she is fragile and scared.

She has seen a lot in life,

But more than the surface,

She has seen the core, the soul;

And once you see that,

You can never see the world the same ever again.

I walk in my soul,

Not just seeing the world, but feeling it.

And while many rush by, living in their heads,

I step slowly, gently, intentionally, as my soul

wanders through this universe.

And I can sense when others are living in

their souls too,

for we share a special bond already.

A secret that only we know.

For if everyone knew about the magic of the soul,

We'd all be walking slower.

Sometimes I sit in the grass and watch

as the world speeds by.

Going to this place or that.

Working, supporting, socializing.

When did life become such a chore?

And as I sit and watch the world speed by,

I'm reminded,

That while everything around me may be moving
quickly,

I can stay still,

And in so doing,

I'm the one moving quickly actually.

For I am growing quickly within as I confront my
traumas,

My insecurities.

So while you rush by, world,

Offering distractions and to-dos that make us not deal
with what truly matters,

I will sit here. Still. And absorb this moment

Completely and Fully.

We emerged from the same crumbled stone.

Knocked down and battered,

We pushed past the rubble and clawed our way

out of the debris.

We look into each other's eyes and see the

pain of the past.

But more than that, we see the survivor.

We see the struggle and the victory.

Perhaps that is why we are drawn together,

For those that did not emerge from the stone

Know not, and never will.

But we who came from the crumbled foundation

Know what it means to fight to be free.

A letter to my younger self:

You don't need to take care of everyone,

They will be okay.

Enjoy your childhood, you'll never get it back.

Life isn't all about winning and achievements.

Stop and watch the clouds, laugh with your friends.

Say yes to love,

but listen to your heart when you know you deserve more.

Don't go out seeking male validation

just because you are sad,

you are enough.

You can be honest with those you love,

They can handle the truth.

Things will get easier, even if it doesn't feel like it now.

Enjoy every moment, even the bad,

For how amazing it is that we live in a world

Where we can experience all these emotions,

And you will never get this moment back.

And don't forget how much I love you.

Faith is to believe without evidence.

"Have faith," he says.

"in what?" I ask.

"In yourself."

Healing the pain of yesterday is the first step

toward moving forward in today.

I numbed and avoided for so long,

But today, I decided to confront my yesterday,

So I can start building a better tomorrow,

Today.

Best intentions can't compete against misperceptions.

Try as you might, it matters less than the reception.

Self love sneaks up on you.

She doesn't flaunt or flirt with you.

But she's been watching you, from a distance.

For many months.

She knows your favorites. Your go-to and types.

She doesn't interfere right away or question your choices.

No, you are free to be you.

And after awhile, when she thinks you will be kind to her,

She will introduce herself to you.

You will be friends at first.

You'll go to yoga with her and do face masks.

But one day, you'll open up to her.

And she will not judge or criticize.

She will listen and offer words of healing.

Later, she will start telling you what you need to hear,

Even before you mention it.

And at last, she will come in

And show you,

New favorites and types,

Steering you away from your past,

Towards a brighter future.

And all because you smiled at her,

When she crept up on you from behind.

Love shouldn't be hard.

Love shouldn't hurt.

Love shouldn't feel forced.

Love should be a joy.

Love should be a gift.

And that's how I know it's not supposed to be

with You anymore.

I met myself today, for the first time in quite a long time.

"How much you have changed," said I.

And as I looked upon this beautiful, strong woman

In front of me,

I was proud. Finally.

I felt love—unlike any love I have ever felt before.

No man will ever compare.

For I have all love for you—me—

Familial, philia, pragma, éros, ludus, philautia,

It's all there, so intense, so pure.

And it took us a long time,

But here we are.

And I'll never leave you again.

9 798999 782318